COMING TO AMERICA
THE WEST INDIAN-AMERICAN EXPERIENCE

BY WARREN J. HALLIBURTON
III

Consultant:
James Shenton
Professor of History
Columbia University

Coming to America
The Millbrook Press
Brookfield, Connecticut

Library of Congress Cataloging-in-Publication Data
Halliburton, Warren J.
The West Indian-American experience/by Warren J. Halliburton.
p.   cm. — (Coming to America)
Includes bibliographical references and index.
Summary: Traces the history of West Indian immigration to the
United States, discussing why they emigrated, their problems in
a new land, and their contributions to American culture.
ISBN 1-56294-340-5 (lib. bdg.)
1. West Indian Americans—History—Juvenile literature.
[1. West Indian Americans—History]   I. Title   II. Series.
E184.W54H35   1994
973'.04969729—dc20   93-19233   CIP   AC

Cover photo courtesy of the Library of Congress

Photos courtesy of Superstock: p. 8; Impact Visuals: pp. 10
(Liza Green), 13 (Donna DeCesare), 52 (Brian Palmer), 56 (Cindy
Reiman); Bettmann: pp. 17, 22, 35, 58 (both); Library of Con-
gress: p. 18; The Granger Collection: pp. 24, 29; New York Public
Library Picture Collection: p. 26, 41, 46, 50; AP/Wide World
Photos p. 47; National Museum of American Art, Washington,
D.C./Art Resource, New York: p. 49. Map by Joe LeMonnier.

Published by The Millbrook Press
2 Old New Milford Road, Brookfield, Connecticut 06804

CONTENTS

INTRODUCTION

"The blood of all the world's peoples flows in the veins of Americans," the author Herman Melville wrote more than a century ago. "A vast ingathering from every continent, Americans have shared the common denominator of being, in most instances, either immigrants or the descendants of immigrants."

In our time, no less than in Melville's, the United States is a nation of immigrants. Each year hundreds of thousands of people pull up stakes and come to America, most of them in search of a new home. On the streets of American cities it is common to hear spoken Polish, Korean, Chinese, Italian, Spanish, and scores of other languages.

Like a great magnet, the United States has drawn those whose lives in other places have been filled with misery. Near-landless peasants of Europe, Latin America, and Asia, oppressed Jews of Eastern Europe, and political outcasts from dictatorships all over the world have fled their homelands for the United States. "The people I knew believed that America was the last place in the world where we could find freedom," said a recent refugee from Eastern Europe.

Here in America, people have overcome their ethnic differences. This has been true since the very beginning of our national history. "I could point out to you," wrote the French immigrant Michel Guillaume Jean de Crèvecoeur in 1782, "a man whose grandfather was an Englishman, whose wife was Dutch, whose son married a French woman, and whose present four sons have now four wives of different nations."

The story of American immigration has unfortunate chapters as well. The ancestors of African Americans, for instance, came to the United States not bound for freedom, but bound by chains and condemned to the horrors of slavery. Nearly every immigrant has encountered discrimination, prejudice, and, all too frequently, outright violence. Sometimes the laws of the United States supported this discrimination. For a long time, people from Asia were turned away from American shores, and refugees from tyranny were sent back to their homelands.

This book is about West Indian Americans, immigrants from what was once the British West Indies in the Caribbean. Beginning about 1900, West Indians began coming to the United States in significant numbers. Like people from every other immigrant group, most West Indians were looking for economic opportunity. That they found. But they paid a dear price for their jobs and new prosperity. Since most were black, West Indian Americans suffered from the cruelty of racial prejudice. The bigotry and discrimination they faced in America was of an intensity unknown in the West Indies. But West Indian Americans did not surrender to prejudice, and because of their courage and determination the United States has become a freer, more tolerant nation.

AN IMMIGRANT'S STORY | 1

On a bright, warm day in October 1989, hundreds of people crowded into an airport terminal in Kingston, Jamaica. Some were tanned and well-dressed American tourists leaving the island after a vacation. Others in the airport were native Jamaicans. They, too, were leaving the island. But their departures had nothing to do with vacations. They were leaving to find new lives in the United States.

Among these Jamaicans was Patricia Dunlap.* Near the departure gate for her flight to New York, she hugged and kissed her family good-bye. She had mixed emotions. Part of her regretted every step she was taking away from Jamaica. But her sadness was mingled with a sense of hope. With all her heart she hoped that a more prosperous life awaited her in the United States. That was what kept her going.

Patricia Dunlap was leaving behind her husband, a son, and three daughters. She told herself that before long all of

---

* The Dunlaps are a composite of all the families the author has read about or known firsthand.

them would be living together in New York City. She would find a way for that reunion to happen.

Something had to be done. The only thing Jamaica offered Patricia and her family was poverty. In Jamaica very few people prospered. White people were nearly always well off. Some mulattos, or those of mixed African and European descent, had also done well for themselves. However, the vast majority of Jamaicans were black. And the vast majority of them were desperately poor. For them there was little hope and scarcely any work.

It was the same story throughout the Caribbean. Whether husking sugarcane on other people's farms or scrubbing floors in other people's kitchens, black Caribbeans simply did not make enough money to get by.

The Dunlap family lived as tenants on a tiny plot of land. Their three-room hut did not compare with the large, solid homes of the landowners. Yet life in the country was better than in the city. There, thousands of poor people crowded into shantytowns and survived by eating scraps of food.

Patricia Dunlap's family had once harvested enough crops both to feed themselves and to have something to sell at the market. But year after year their land became less and less productive. No matter how hard the Dunlaps worked, they were able to raise only a few garden vegetables. Quite simply, their plot was worn out.

The Dunlaps could no longer afford to live together as a family. Patricia took whatever work was available outside the home, usually as a maid. Mister Dunlap, as Patricia called her husband, was seldom around. He would hear there was work somewhere—on Jamaica or on another island—and he would be off. His jobs were many and varied. He did everything from working at a bauxite refinery to helping dig the foundation for a new tourist hotel.

A beachside resort in Jamaica. Like many of the Caribbean islands, Jamaica is a popular vacation spot for tourists from the United States and elsewhere.

With their parents working all the time, the Dunlaps' children were often left on their own. Their son Roger was at loose ends. When he turned sixteen he had dropped out of school. In the year since, he spent all his days and many of his nights away from home. He did not have a job.

The three girls—Carmen, Joyce, and Doreen—stayed in school. They were expected to do their homework, which they did. They were also supposed to do housework. But only fifteen-year-old Carmen, the eldest girl, helped with the cooking and cleaning.

There had to be a better way. Talking to friends and neighbors, Patricia heard about Jamaican families who had left the island for the United States and a more prosperous way of life.

Gradually Patricia worked out a plan. She would go to New York City by herself. She would find work and a place to live. She would save her money. When she had saved enough she would send for her husband and children.

It was not easy to move to the United States. Patricia had to comply with the American laws regulating immigration. The simplest way would be to have relatives in the United States. Then she could be sponsored by them. But all of Patricia's family lived in Jamaica.

There was another way. She could be sponsored by an American citizen who promised to give her a job. Patricia got in touch with a friend of a friend who lived in New York, a Mrs. Myers. As luck would have it, Mrs. Myers knew a woman who was looking for a housekeeper. This was Patricia's opening. The woman agreed to hire Patricia and sponsor her immigration to the United States.

Through the spring and summer of 1989, Patricia fulfilled the official requirements for immigration. She obtained a work permit and a visa. Meanwhile, her future employer worked with American immigration officials in New York. By late September of 1989, the wait was over. Patricia Dunlap was granted clearance for a green card, the document allowing noncitizens to work in the United States. Finally, she was on her way.

New York City came as a shock. No one had prepared Patricia for what the city would be like. The weather was colder than she had imagined October could be. People told her that she had not seen anything yet. "Wait until January," they said.

At least she understood most New Yorkers when they talked. Unlike many immigrants, Patricia spoke English. This was a considerable advantage, one that had always helped immigrants from the English-speaking West Indies.

Patricia's new home was in Brooklyn, one of the five boroughs, or sections, of New York City. She lived in the maid's room of her new employer's apartment. The room was small and sparsely furnished. Her employer was demanding, her children rude, her husband unfriendly, and the apartment itself was cluttered with furniture that always needed dusting.

On her day off each week, Patricia explored the city. That meant riding the underground trains of the subway, dodging traffic, and riding buses. At first she kept to the mostly black neighborhoods of Brooklyn. She saw that she had not left poverty behind in Jamaica. At every turn, she noticed run-down buildings, vacant stores, and unemployed men and women. It was also dangerous. She heard horrible stories about shootings, robberies, and drug dealing.

Patricia discovered whole neighborhoods of Jamaicans and others from the West Indies. Grocery stores in these parts of town carried items from her homeland such as spiced bread, peanut punch, calypso sauce, goat meat, and oxtail soup. In the evenings, West Indians crowded into nightclubs such as the Tilden Ballroom in Brooklyn, the Reggae Lounge across the East River in Manhattan, and the Q Club in Queens. There they listened to the calypso and reggae music born in the West Indies. Many of the clubs, restaurants, and stores were owned by West Indian immigrants. Patricia saw this as convincing proof that it was possible to get ahead in America.

Patricia worked and scrimped and saved for two years. At last she was able to send for her family. They arrived together, tear-stained and starry-eyed, in the fall of 1991. Seeing their happy faces and sharing in their excitement, Patricia felt certain that she had made the right decision in leaving Jamaica.

A month before their arrival Patricia had started looking for a place to live. She had found a five-room apartment on the top floor of an old building in Brooklyn. The neighborhood

Like Patricia Dunlap, the West Indian woman in this photo found work in the United States as a nanny and housekeeper.

was not the best, and she was suspicious of the other tenants in the building, but for the time being it would do.

Mr. Dunlap found work as a supply clerk in a tool factory. But one job was not enough. Soon he found a second job, cleaning floors in an office building. And then he located a third job, this one as night watchman for a shipping depot on the Brooklyn waterfront. For a while, Patricia kept her old housekeeping job. In time, though, she found better work as a matron in a hospital. Her duties included making beds, changing laundry, and emptying bedpans.

Patricia enrolled her three daughters in public schools— Carmen in high school, Joyce at the local junior high, and Doreen in a nearby elementary school. Roger, now eighteen, had more difficulty adjusting than his sisters. He lost interest in continuing his education and resumed his old ways. Often he was nowhere to be found.

So, for the Dunlaps, some things had not changed. The three girls still went to school and still argued over the housework. Mr. Dunlap was still away most of the time working his three jobs. Patricia was still cleaning up after other people, and Roger was still at loose ends.

A few things had changed for the worse. In America racial prejudice was worse than in Jamaica. In Jamaica, people looked down on the Dunlaps for being poor. In New York, Patricia and her family were scorned for being black. It was a painful experience.

But when all was said and done, America, a rich and powerful country, offered them the promise of a better life. For the first time in their lives the Dunlaps had the chance to make good and to escape the pitfalls of poverty. And that was why they had come to America.

THE WEST INDIES | 2

The term "West Indian" usually refers to people from the English-speaking Caribbean, or from those places that were once colonies of Great Britain. The former British West Indies have a good deal in common with neighboring places such as Puerto Rico and the Dominican Republic where Spanish is the principal language, and islands such as Martinique and Guadeloupe where French is spoken. Many immigrants stress these similarities by calling themselves "Caribbean" rather than West Indian.

Nevertheless, the English-speaking people from the Caribbean are bound by history, language, custom, and the pattern of their immigration to the United States.

They also share another heritage. Although West Indians were born in the Caribbean islands, most of their ancestors came from Africa, from the present-day countries of Sierra Leone, Guinea, Ghana, the Ivory Coast, Nigeria, and elsewhere. This part of the West Indian experience involves one of the great tragedies in human history—that of slavery.

Columbus's Mistake ▪ The West Indies form a long chain of islands that separates the Caribbean Sea from the Atlantic Ocean. The islands stretch in a graceful 2,000-mile (3,218-kilometer) arc from the Bahamas off the coast of Florida to Trinidad and Tobago just east of Venezuela in South America.

The islands are divided into groups according to their location: The Bahamas lie in the north, the Greater Antilles near the center, and the Lesser Antilles in the southeast. The Greater Antilles includes the large islands of Cuba, Jamaica, Hispaniola, and Puerto Rico. The Lesser Antilles are the smaller islands in the chain. The northern group of the Lesser Antilles is called the Leeward Islands, and the southern group the Windward Islands.

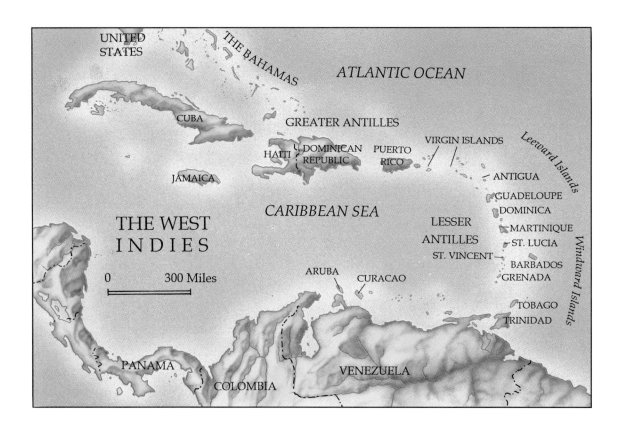

In this lithograph, Columbus kneels in thanksgiving for having reached the Indies. In fact, he had reached what is now Watling Island in the Bahamas.

The West Indies received their name because of a mistake made by Christopher Columbus. When the great navigator sailed westward from Spain in August 1492, he hoped to find a new route to the Indies, which at that time meant India, China, Indonesia, and Japan. When, in October 1492, he and his crew set foot on what is now Watling Island in the Bahamas, they had no idea that they were on the doorstep of a vast continent unknown to Europeans. Columbus thought he was near Japan or China. The people he encountered on the islands of the Caribbean were, he insisted, Indians. Within thirty years everyone knew that Columbus was wrong. But his name for the people and place stuck. The native inhabitants of America came to be called Indians, and the islands of the Caribbean the West Indies.

THE ARAWAKS

Although the original inhabitants of the Caribbean, the Arawaks, were wiped out by European settlers, traces of their culture remain. For example, pepperpot stew, an Arawak dish, is still served. It is a stew made with vegetables, red pepper, and meat.

Familiar words also come from the Arawak language. The Arawak word *huracan* is, in English, "hurricane," *tobaco* is "tobacco," *canaua* is "canoe," and *hamaca* is "hammock."

Many Arawak phrases, when translated, are wonderfully descriptive. For instance, the Arawaks referred to the thumb as "father of the fingers," the pulse as "soul of the hand," and a rainbow as "God's plume of feathers." They called an earthquake "the boiling pot," and an Arawak man often referred to his wife as "my heart."

Arawaks making bread.

The Caribbean islands had a long history prior to 1492. Cibony Indians were probably the first people to inhabit the West Indies. They migrated from South America to the island of Hispaniola. Those settling along the coast became fishermen, and those who ventured inland became hunters.

The Cibony were followed by the Arawaks, who also traveled northward from South America. They settled in the Bahamas and the Greater Antilles and became farmers.

Sometime in the 1300s another group—the Caribs—migrated from South America. They first settled in the western part of Cuba. Unlike the Arawaks, the Caribs were warlike. They raided Arawak villages in the Greater Antilles and eventually ruled over most of the Arawaks in the region.

Laying Claim ▪ When Christopher Columbus led his sailors to the shores of the New World, the old way of West Indian life began to change for good. Between 1492 and 1502, Columbus made four voyages to the West Indies, claiming each island he explored as Spanish territory. For the following 130 years Spain would rule the Caribbean.

The excitement of a new world appealed to other Spanish adventurers. They had heard stories about gold and other riches awaiting those bold enough to make the voyage. Hundreds responded and became the first European colonists in the New World. Their arrival was the beginning of the end for the Caribbean civilization.

Indians were the victims of European exploitation. Forced into slavery, many died from overwork and despair. Many more died from European diseases such as smallpox, measles, influenza, and malaria. Within 150 years of Columbus's first voyage, nearly all the Indian population of the Caribbean had perished.

The loss of these native people did not particularly grieve the Spanish. They were too busy pursuing wealth. But the

West Indies did not have much of the wealth the Spanish were looking for. With their vast deposits of gold, Mexico and South America were the jewels of the Spanish Empire. For the Spanish, the West Indies became something of a neglected backwater, used mainly as places from which to defend their sea routes to Central and South America.

In the early 1600s, Spain's European enemies—the English, French, and Dutch—began eyeing the West Indies. Scrambling for any foothold in the global struggle against the Spanish Empire, these powers seized many of the lightly defended islands of the Caribbean.

England got the biggest share. The English established a colony on the island of St. Christopher in 1623. Two years later they took possession of Barbados, and in 1628 they occupied Nevis in the Leeward Islands. In 1655 an English expedition captured Jamaica from the Spanish.

Sugar and Slavery • When the English took over, the West Indies were neither prosperous nor populous. Jamaica had a population of only three thousand people. Barbados was virtually uninhabited. Disease had wiped out the Indian population, and when the English arrived on the island they noticed only a flourishing population of wild hogs.

The first English settlers were mainly interested in farming, and they grew mostly tobacco and cotton on small plots of land. They did not have much luck. Although the soil was rich and the sun was bright, their tobacco was not of very good quality. The farmers struggled to get by.

That did not last long. "There is a great change on this island of late," wrote a resident of Barbados in 1646, "from worse to better, praise be God." This "great change" was the transition to growing sugarcane.

Europeans in those days possessed a sweet tooth that seemed never to be satisfied. The demand for sugar and products made from sugar, such as rum and molasses, was enormous. The tropical climate of the West Indies proved ideal for the cultivation of sugarcane. Overnight, the islands became tremendously valuable. In 1646 a single sugar plantation on Barbados sold for 16,000 English pounds. A few years before, the entire *island* could have been purchased for less.

Growing sugarcane efficiently required two things, lots of land and lots of labor. The need for land was solved by creating sprawling sugar plantations. By 1680 over half the land on Barbados, the first island converted to sugar production, was occupied by just 175 large sugar plantations.

The need for labor was solved by slavery. There had been slaves in the West Indies nearly as long as there had been Europeans. In 1518 the Spanish brought the first African slaves to the Caribbean. They were needed, the Spanish insisted, to do the hard work that the dwindling Indian population could no longer do. When the English seized Jamaica in 1655, over 1,500 African slaves were held by the Spanish rulers of the island.

As sugarcane cultivation spread from island to island the demand for labor soared. To work the cane fields, mills, distilleries, and boiling houses, the plantation owners, or planters, purchased more and more slaves. The slave trade became a large and profitable business. For two hundred years, from the mid-1600s until the 1830s, more than 1,500,000 slaves from Africa arrived in the West Indies.

The slave trade involved acquiring and selling human beings. Operating in West Africa, European slave merchants managed to capture young Africans. Often chained to one another, the newly enslaved people were brutally driven to the coast where they were eventually packed into the filthy and cramped holds of slave ships for the trip to the West Indies. The slow trip could last as long as three months. This dreadful voyage came to be called "the middle passage."

A century and a half after Columbus's landfall, sugar production in the Caribbean provided Europeans with windfall profits. This engraving shows a laborer tending sugarcane.

On their arrival in the West Indies, slaves were put ashore and placed on display. Presented at the auction block, they were now for sale to the highest bidders.

The horrors of slavery and the middle passage are seared deeply into the life and culture of the West Indies. Even today they are remembered and lamented. As the Jamaican reggae singer Bob Marley sang shortly before his death in 1981:

Old pirates, yes they rob I
Sold I to the merchant's ships
Minutes after they took I
from the bottomless pit . . . .

FROM SLAVERY TO FREEDOM | 3

During the eighteenth century, the world's demand for sugar continued to grow, and the West Indies became its premier supplier. As might be expected, the demand for slaves increased as well. In the 1700s the population of the West Indies became overwhelmingly African. On most islands, more than 90 percent of the population was black and more than 90 percent of them were enslaved.

Life on the Sugar Plantations ▪ The owners of the great West Indian sugar plantations grew very rich. But for all their wealth few were happy. Most had come from England, and life in the tropical West Indies was different from what they were accustomed to. Many homesick planters returned to England where they became absentee landlords.

In their absence, many plantations fell to ruin. Over the years the repeated planting of sugarcane took its toll. As the soil grew poorer, it became harder to produce an abundant crop. The planters had a simple solution to this problem: To make a profit, they worked their slaves to death.

A sugar plantation on the island of St. Croix.

On a typical sugar plantation, slaves lived in floorless huts. They worked six days a week, twelve hours a day. Their day began before sunrise when they were given a cup of ginger tea and sent into the cane fields. Children, pregnant women, and nursing mothers were given less difficult jobs. Any disobedience was met with swift, brutal punishment—often a beating, which might result in death.

Many slave owners did not consider their slaves to be quite human. On Grenada the British governor appointed a "Superintendent of all the Negroes, and Mules or Horses which are furnished for His Majesty's Service in this island." And, like a horse or mule, an enslaved person was often branded with his owner's mark or initials.

This drawing, ironically titled "West Indian Philanthropy" (goodwill), shows a plantation owner whipping a slave for daring to talk of freedom.

Faced with this inhuman brutality, enslaved people created a distinctive life and culture. Most West Indian slaves lived as families. And, as families, they revived age-old African traditions. These included religious ceremonies as well as festivals, which they celebrated with music and dance.

They also developed a way of communicating among themselves. Slave songs became a common language. A mix of English words and African expressions conveyed messages that non-Africans could not understand.

But slaves were denied any formal education and forbidden to worship in their own way. Many were converted by the English to Christianity. In their worship, slaves combined Christian elements with West African spirits. Out of this mix, a variety of Afro-Christian worship emerged.

"Unappropriated People" ▪ Although they lived among themselves, slaves often had relationships with whites. These affairs were neither encouraged nor condemned by West Indian society. They simply happened, as did the mulatto children born from these unions.

The mulattos grew into a distinct social class. Some remained in slavery, but a considerable number were granted freedom. Freedom did not mean equality with whites, however. "There is . . . a third description of people," wrote the Governor of Barbados in 1802, "these are the Black and colored people who are not slaves, and yet whom I cannot bring myself to call free. I think *unappropriated people* would be a more proper denomination for them, for though not the property of other individuals they do not enjoy the shadow of any civil right."

By the 1830s more than 10 percent of the population of Jamaica and Barbados were of this "third description"—free nonwhites.

Rebellion ▪ Never content with lives of bondage, slaves again and again planned and plotted revolts against the colonial regime. Between 1640 and 1713 at least seven slave revolts broke out in the British islands. Six major conspiracies were also discovered in their planning stages.

The most serious slave rebellions occurred in Jamaica, the largest of the British-held islands. With its dense forests and rugged mountains, Jamaica offered the hiding places necessary for a revolt to have any hope of success.

In 1760 an upheaval known as Tacky's Rebellion broke out. Its leader, Tacky, who had been a tribal chief in Africa prior to his enslavement, gathered a small party of trusted followers and carefully laid plans for an insurrection. On Easter Monday, 1760, they overpowered a British fort and made off with a supply of muskets and ammunition. Hundreds of slaves joined as Tacky led his armed band onto the plantations. There they killed many astonished whites.

Eventually more than one thousand slaves entered the rebellion. British troops and the local militia fought back fiercely. In several months of on-and-off fighting, about sixty whites and between three hundred and four hundred black slaves were killed. Tacky himself was shot down after he and his most loyal cohorts had escaped to the wooded countryside. Other leaders of the rebellion were publicly executed; two were burned alive, and two were hung in iron cages and starved to death.

The brutal suppression of Tacky's Rebellion calmed matters down only temporarily. Many slaves were prepared to die rather than continue to endure their miserable existence. Revolts continued to erupt. In 1816, for example, slaves in Barbados exploded in insurrection, setting fire to the island's sugarcane crop. The rebellion failed, leaving 176 blacks dead. Another 214 were executed for taking part in the affair.

West Indian slaves continued not only to talk of freedom but to risk their lives for it. Shown here is a slave revolt on Hispaniola.

"As Free as Ourselves" ▪ By the early 1800s, unforeseen events lent a helping hand to the slaves. The sugar plantations of the West Indies were in serious trouble. The demand for West Indian sugar, once so powerful, had weakened. The sugar beet, a plant that could be grown in Europe, had taken over enough of the market to threaten the riches that had once come so abundantly from sugarcane.

With sugarcane in decline, the system of plantation slavery became too costly to support. Rebellions and insurrections added to the problem. Jamaica, wrote a settler in the early 1800s, was "more like a garrison . . . than a country of commerce and agriculture."

In Great Britain a strong antislavery, or abolitionist, movement emerged. Led by William Wilberforce, a British statesman, abolitionists denounced slavery as cruel and inhumane and as having no place in the British Empire. Their humanitarian arguments were persuasive; in 1807 the British Parliament abolished the slave trade. From then on, slaves could no longer be legally brought from Africa into any part of the British Empire.

The slaves themselves delivered the final blows to slavery in the West Indies. Just after Christmas in 1831, Jamaica erupted in a slave revolt, the most widespread in the island's history. It was now plain that the enslaved people of the West Indies would accept nothing less than freedom. At long last, in 1833, Parliament abolished the institution of slavery. In 1838, after a four-year period of transition, the slaves of the British Empire were set free.

On the day freedom finally came, William Hart Coleridge, a prominent English minister and abolitionist in Barbados, wrote:

> 800,000 human beings lay down last night as slaves, and rose in the morning as free as ourselves. . . . It was

my peculiar happiness on that ever memorable day to address a congregation of nearly 4,000 people, of whom more than 3,000 were Negroes just emancipated. And such was the order, the deep attention, and perfect silence, that you might have heard a pin drop.

Homes in the Hills ▪ Coleridge offered his respectful audience some advice. He urged the former slaves to stand by their former masters. "You owe it to them as God's deputies to obey their orders even though you are no longer slaves," he said.

This was certainly what the masters wanted to hear. To keep their plantations going, they needed the same amount of labor as before, and they were willing to pay their former slaves for it—but not much. On Barbados and other small islands, the newly freed slaves had little choice but to take what was offered. Nearly all the land on these islands was owned by a few planters.

In Jamaica it was a different story. There the former slaves had a choice, and few chose to work for their former masters. Most left the plantations to which they had been bound and moved to the hilly land rejected by planters.

In the hills the former slaves established their own settlements, built huts, and started farms. They planted root crops, vegetables, and corn. Most of these crops were raised for themselves, but whenever they had a surplus, they sold it at plantation markets.

It was a hard life. Many farmers did not make it and were forced to return to the plantations, where they worked for pitifully low wages.

Too few returned to satisfy the planters' demands for labor. To make up the difference the colonial governments of the West Indies began to import laborers from India, China, and Africa. They came as indentured servants under a contract to work for a given period of time. Once they had fulfilled this commitment, these workers became free immigrants. Between 1838 and 1917, nearly 500,000 people from India, then part of the British Empire, came to work on West Indian sugar plantations. The greatest number, 145,000, went to Trinidad, an island the British had captured from Spain in 1797. These new immigrants brought a new racial, cultural, and religious diversity to the West Indies. The Indians held to their Muslim and Hindu beliefs and built mosques and temples in the cities of the Caribbean. The Chinese often became merchants. By 1900, Chinese-owned corner grocery stores were a common sight in nearly every West Indian town.

LEAVING HOME | 4

In the years following the end of slavery, West Indians settled into a new way of life. The population was divided into three broad classes. The upper class was white. As the descendants of slave owners, whites continued to own most of the land and to make most of the money.

Over time a middle class emerged. Some were merchants, others were teachers, professional people, and civil servants. The British government realized that their colonies could not function without trained personnel, and they needed more than would ever come from England. Local inhabitants were therefore enlisted and educated to perform the functions of government. They policed the streets, ran the schools, and worked in government offices. This middle class consisted mainly of mulattos.

By far the largest of the groups in West Indian society were the black masses, the former slaves and their descendants. Most were peasants. Their efforts to survive as independent farmers often failed. Tens of thousands left their farms in desperation to find work in nearby cities. Those fortunate enough to find jobs labored under the worst conditions. Workplaces were generally filthy, and the pay was barely enough to live on. Worse, there were not enough jobs to go around.

There were a few bright spots. One was education. The West Indies had among the highest literacy rates in the world, higher than the United States and most European countries. On Barbados, for instance, more than 90 percent of the population could read and write. A woman from Barbados recalled:

> Schooling is important on the islands. Teachers and parents are allied against children. "You are to pay attention and learn," children are told sternly. Teachers are free to whip children, and use that freedom liberally. If a child comes home and reports that the teacher hit him, he can expect another beating, probably on his bare bottom . . . . I got my share of floggings, and it produced the effect that was desired. I went to school to pay attention and to learn.[1]

"Panama Man" ▪ What practical good was an education, though, if there were so few jobs? Between 1896 and 1936 the population of the British West Indies grew by 50 percent. This dramatic increase was too much for the small islands. If people were to find work they would have to find it elsewhere.

A few went to Great Britain, the mother country of the colonies. Others went to Cuba and found work on sugar and coffee plantations. Panama, in Central America, was a magnet. Between 1881 and 1914, 100,000 men, mostly from Jamaica and Barbados, emigrated to Panama. There, they helped to build the canal which, when finished, would connect the Atlantic with the Pacific. The "Panama Man" grew into a legend on some islands. He was the fellow who returned from Panama wearing fine new clothes and flashing a big roll

Construction of the Panama Canal provided many West Indians with job opportunities. This photo shows workers with hydraulic drills helping to build the canal.

of American dollars. But those who came back broke were scorned by their family and girlfriends. "Oh de Panama man ain't got no money, Still de Panama man want love," went the verse of a popular folk song.

Looking to America ▪ The greatest opportunities for jobs and a better life lay not in Great Britain or Panama or some other place in the Caribbean. The United States offered the best hope, just as it did for people from Europe and Asia. With its booming industrial economy, the United States had jobs for almost anyone who wanted to work.

During the first quarter of the twentieth century, more and more West Indians boarded steamships in Caribbean ports and sailed for Florida, Massachusetts, and, most of all, New York City. In 1899 just 412 immigrants from the West Indies were admitted to the United States. The number rose to 5,633 in 1907. In 1924 it swelled to 12,243. By 1930, well over 150,000 West Indian immigrants and their children were living in the United States.

It was not just the poor who left their homes for the United States. Middle-class people, most of whom were mulattos, arrived in large numbers. Between 1911 and 1924, 71 percent of West Indian immigrants were either professional people, office workers, or skilled laborers. Whatever their class, the newcomers were educated. Fully 99 percent could read and write English. In contrast, only about two thirds of the immigrants from Europe could read or write any language at all.

Bitter Medicine ▪ "The city was so different from the island," recalled Congresswoman Shirley Chisholm, who as a girl of eleven came to New York City from Barbados, where she had spent her childhood. "I kept getting lost. When Mother sent me on short errands, I got mixed up at the corners. . . . I couldn't get used to keeping on the sidewalk, either. When it was crowded I would take to the street, and Mother would scold, 'Shirley, you gonna get killed someday.' "

But the hardest thing to get used to was not the crowded sidewalks or the miles and miles of paved streets. It was the bitter reality of American racism.

"I wasn't aware of my color till I got here, honestly," said an immigrant from Jamaica. He knew, of course, that his skin was black in Jamaica. But nothing there prepared him for the indignities he would suffer as a black man in the United States.

In the West Indies, where more than 90 percent of the population was African, blacks were part of a great majority. In the United States, 90 percent of the population was white, and blacks were a persecuted minority. In the southern states, where most African Americans lived, blacks went to separate schools, were often denied the right to vote, could not serve on juries, and were legally separated from whites in public places such as theaters, parks, and railway cars. It was not until the 1960s that this system of legal segregation, or separation by race, was dismantled. Large northern cities lacked southern-style legal segregation. But, in practice, New York City was just as segregated as Birmingham, Alabama. New York landlords refused to rent apartments to blacks in white neighborhoods, and many stores and restaurants in midtown Manhattan closed their doors to black patrons.

Like African Americans, immigrants from the West Indies faced discrimination and prejudice in seeking employment, on the job, and in their social lives. The United States was a rich country, and most West Indian immigrants found the jobs and income they were looking for. But they paid a steep price for their economic well-being—they joined the ranks of America's oppressed.

"SHE FORGOT ABOUT SHOES"

In 1919, Lunan Ferguson, a young man from a middle-class Jamaican family, sailed to New York, where he was reunited with his mother. He had not seen her for more than eight years.

Years later he recalled the experience:

My youngest aunt, my mother's twenty-four-year-old sister, wanted to come with me to America. Her family didn't have the money to give her for passage, so Mother had to . . . save the ship's passage money and the $200 "show money" for her . . . . Foreigners had to have that show money to assure the officials at Ellis Island [the place in New York harbor where immigrants to the United States were either admitted or rejected] that we were not paupers and would not become public charges. It took my mother another whole year to save that money for my aunt and me . . . .

My aunt and I traveled to Kingston [the capital of Jamaica] to prepare to take ship to America. We had to get passports, and to undergo a thorough physical examination. Among other things, we would-be passengers had to submit to the American Embassy doctor a specimen of our feces to see if we harbored hookworm or any other intestinal parasites. They told us to bring the specimen in a matchbox. We did. But lo and behold, my aunt, a very prissy young lady of twenty-four, thought it beneath her dignity to do so herself, so she had one of the servants of our relatives in Kingston at whose house we stayed take care of this little chore for her . . . .

Our steamer, the SS Carillo, a United Fruit Company steamer, left Kingston on December 13, 1919, and arrived at Ellis Island on December 19, 1919. . . .

Well, my aunt and I landed in Ellis Island and were processed before being allowed to go ashore. Mother had sent us passage money and "show money" in a package. She sent a registered package with many large U.S. bills and $100 in gold coins for me to show. So I proudly flourished my five $20 gold pieces to the immigration officials. Mother was waiting for us. I would not have known her, because the last time I saw her I was only seven, in 1911, and I was now a big boy just one month from my sixteenth birthday. My canvas shoes were no protection from the subfreezing weather on that cold December 19 day in New York, and my two big toes got frostbitten.

Mother had brought with her overcoats for my Aunt Amy and me, overshoes, lined woolen gloves, and a fur cap for me. But she forgot about the shoes. [2]

West Indians did not accept their loss of status quietly. In 1918, Raymond Jones, an immigrant from the Virgin Islands, got a job as a porter on a train transporting American servicemen to the South. Before long, he remembered, the soldiers started shouting insults at him:

> "Boy, why did you do this?" "Boy, do that." "Nigger, do this." "Nigger, do that." I was unaccustomed to this kind of harassment and let it be known that I resented these indignities. The southern recruits, however, interpreted my reaction as the show of an uppity Nigger who didn't know his place; when the train reached Georgia, the recruits physically attacked me, thinking, I believe, that the time had come to put me in my "place."[3]

Like Jones, many West Indians resisted being put in their "place." Before long the Pullman Company, which operated the sleeping cars on American railroads, stopped hiring West Indians as porters. This was because, the firm said, "of their refusal to accept insults from passengers quietly."

Living in the Big City ▪ West Indian immigrants to New York City discovered that there were only three neighborhoods in the vast metropolis where they could live: Harlem, in northern Manhattan, and Bedford-Stuyvesant and Crown Heights, in Brooklyn. Everywhere else was for "whites only." By 1930 nearly 40,000 West Indians lived in Harlem. They accounted for about a quarter of the black neighborhood's population.

Although they shared a common African heritage, relations between African Americans and West Indians were distant and sometimes hostile. Both groups were recent immigrants to New York, with African Americans coming in great numbers from the American South in the early years of the

A Harlem promenade during the 1920s. At that time, pride was on the rise among the area's black residents. Relations between the West Indians and African Americans living there were, however, often strained.

twentieth century. Tension frequently flared between these two immigrant groups living in close quarters on the streets of Harlem. West Indians were often ridiculed for their British accents and elaborate tropical clothing. African Americans criticized West Indians for being pushy, clannish, and self-centered. They were called by such names as "monkey-chaser," "ring-tale," "king mon," and "cockney." Children took to throwing stones and taunting West Indians for their different ways. A popular verse of the day went:

When a monkey-chaser dies
Don't need no undertaker;
Just throw him in the Harlem River,
He'll float back to Jamaica.

West Indians and African Americans prayed differently, too. The majority of African Americans were Baptists and Methodists. The majority of West Indians were members of the Anglican Church of England. The quiet reserve of West Indian worship contrasted with the spirited worship at African-American services.

Families, too, were different. African Americans considered West Indian families too formal and straitlaced. West Indians took their formal behavior for granted. As slaves, their families had been allowed to remain together. Through the years, the West Indian father had become the dominant figure at home, the key worker and wage earner. In the United States, marriage between slaves was illegal, and slave families were often broken up. Since the father in a family was often forced out, the mother became the dominant figure in the household.

The distrust between the two groups did not go away. People tended to forget what they had in common and to stress their differences. One prominent West Indian argued that his people were "almost totally different" from the "average rural negro from the South." An African American succinctly replied to this sort of criticism: "If you West Indians don't like how we do things in this country, you should go back where you came from . . . ."

A CALL TO ARMS 5

West Indian immigrants to the United States held tightly to the British traditions they had grown up with in the Caribbean. In May 1937, more than five thousand West Indians jammed a Harlem ballroom to celebrate the coronation of King George VI. And in fair weather or foul, in the parks and open spaces of northern Manhattan, West Indians expertly and joyfully played the mysterious English game of cricket.

By and large, West Indian immigrants preferred to remain British subjects rather than become American citizens. Those who did become nationalized were often scorned by their fellow immigrants. Put simply, West Indians did not wish to become citizens of a country that treated blacks so disgracefully.

Remaining loyal to Britain also gave the immigrant a certain small protection against discrimination. "I am a British subject, I will report this to my consulate!" was a common cry of West Indians when faced with racial prejudice. The British consulate in New York was frequently filled with angry people recounting that this movie theater or that restaurant had not admitted them. Unfortunately, there was little that British diplomats could do to alter American racism.

"Pushfulness" ▪ It was a common saying in Harlem that when a West Indian "gets ten cents above a beggar, he opens a business." During the 1920s and 1930s this seemed to be true. Everywhere you looked in Harlem, there were stores and shops owned and operated by emigrants from the West Indies. An African-American journalist, impressed by all this commercial activity, praised the West Indians for their "enterprise in business, their pushfulness."

This "pushfulness" took many forms. Very often a half dozen or so West Indians would pool their savings and buy an apartment building. By renting out the apartments they turned a healthy profit.

They often pooled their money. A dozen or so friends would create a credit association by contributing to a jointly owned fund. Then the fund would be "rotated." This meant that one member of the association was loaned the money to finance his business activities. When business prospered, the debt was repaid, and the money was lent to another person. West Indian women were particularly active in these associations. These women served as bankers and collectors. People said that they "threw a regular hand" to help small businesses get started.

Voices of the Time ▪ During the 1920s, West Indians tried to rally their fellow immigrants. Organizing themselves into various groups, they formed the West Indian Committee on America, the Foreign-Born Citizen's Alliance, and the West Indian Reform Association. All demanded better treatment for blacks.

West Indians became famous as street-corner preachers. Standing on soapboxes and stepladders to be better seen and heard by passers-by, they protested racism in blunt terms.

By the mid-1920s many leading West Indians were calling for greater unity with African Americans. "West Indian Negroes are oppressed. American Negroes are equally oppressed," cried William Bridges, a West Indian immigrant and political organizer. "West Indians, you are black, Americans you are equally black. It is your color upon which white men pass judgment, not your merits, nor the geographic line between you."

Marcus Garvey ▪ In the late summer of 1920 the streets of Harlem were alive with activity. Black people from all over the United States and from twenty-five different countries had come to town for a meeting of the Universal Negro Improvement Association. Marching bands paraded up and down the avenues welcoming the visitors. Newsboys sold special editions of the newspaper *Negro World*. Drugstores and tobacco counters got into the spirit of things by offering a special cigar for the occasion. On the band of the cigar was a color picture of the founder of the organization. He was the man of the hour. His name was Marcus Garvey.

Born in 1887 and raised in a small town on the north coast of Jamaica, Garvey had always resented the mistreatment of black people. He was, in his own words, "determined that the black man would not continue to be kicked about by all the other races and nations of the world."

In 1914, while working as a printer in Jamaica, Garvey founded the Universal Negro Improvement Association, or UNIA. The aim of the organization, he said, was "uniting all the Negro people of the world into one great body to establish a country and government absolutely their own."

Two years later, in March 1916, Garvey came to the United States. Traveling across the country, he and his organization electrified African Americans. By the early 1920s the UNIA had tens of thousands of members and its newspaper a circulation of over 10,000.

Garvey's ultimate goal was to reclaim Africa from the Europeans who had colonized the continent. He also meant to instill in African Americans a sense of pride and racial unity. Using the contributions to the UNIA, Garvey established black-run businesses. He opened a chain of grocery stores, two restaurants, a printing plant, a laundry, and a dressmaking shop. To transport blacks between the West Indies, Africa, and the United States, he established a steamship company, the Black Star Line.

Garvey drew strong support from throughout the black community. His most devoted supporters were West Indians. "They rushed to his standard," one scholar has written. "He was one of their countrymen starting a new and wonderful movement of which no American Negro ever thought."

A UNIA demonstration.

"THE BIG BLACK REPUBLIC"

On the evening of August 2, 1920, more than 25,000 people crowded into Madison Square Garden in New York. Nearly all of them were black. A few had come from Africa for the occasion. Many more were West Indians and African Americans. They were there for the convention of the

Marcus Garvey in uniform as a leader of the "big black republic" he sought to create in Africa.

Universal Negro Improvement Association. And they were there to hear Marcus Garvey speak. In his deep, resonant voice, Garvey addressed the crowd:

The Negroes of the world say, "We are striking homewards towards Africa to make her the big black republic." And in the making of Africa a big black republic, what is the barrier? The barrier is the white man; and we say to the white man who now dominates Africa that it is to his interest to clear out of Africa now, because we are coming not as in the time of Father Abraham, 200,000 strong, but we are coming 400,000,000 strong and we mean to retake every square inch of the 12,000,000 square miles of African territory belonging to us by right Divine. . . . We are out to get what has belonged to us politically, socially, economically, and in every way. . . .

The first dying that is to be done by the black man in the future will be done to make himself free. [4]

Some black leaders had no time for Garvey. They said his goals were hopelessly unrealistic. Others called him a fraud. Chandler Owen, a black labor leader, denounced him as the "mudsill of Jamaican society."

But Garvey's most serious enemies were white. Throughout his career, federal agents had kept watch on his activities, and in 1923 the government indicted him for mail fraud. The case against him involved the financing of the Black Star Line. Despite being honest and sincere, Garvey was convicted and sentenced to five years in prison. Although the sentence was later commuted, Garvey was deported to Jamaica as an undesirable alien. His dream of a world where black people would be independent of whites was in ruins.

The sad fate of Marcus Garvey broke the hearts of many West Indians. Shirley Chisolm remembered that her father talked of his fallen hero all the time: "He seemed almost to worship Garvey and was particularly proud of the fact he was a West Indian, too. Papa believed America had treated Garvey wrongly, and as a result he talked negatively about the country. 'America's got a lot to learn,' Papa often proclaimed."

The Harlem Renaissance • The racial pride that Garvey stirred inspired many black artists and writers. During the 1920s, their works were displayed and published as never before. This outburst of art and literature became known as the Harlem Renaissance. (Renaissance is a French word meaning rebirth, or revival.)

Many of the most influential writers of this movement were West Indian. Among them was the journalist W. A. Domingo. A Jamaican, he defined the "New Negro" as insisting on "absolute and unequivocal equality." He declared that black people should educate themselves and work their way up the economic ladder.

The Harlem Renaissance embraced the work of writers such as Langston Hughes and musicians such as W. C. Handy. This painting, "Man in a Vest," is by William H. Johnson, an artist connected with the Harlem Renaissance.

The idea was supported by many of the writers and artists of the Harlem Renaissance. Among them was Claude McKay, another Jamaican. In his novel *Home To Harlem*, published in 1928, McKay attacked racism and promised the rise of black people to their rightful place in the world.

McKay's poetry explored the same themes. His poem "If We Must Die" spoke of the race riots in Chicago and East St. Louis during and immediately after World War I, conflagrations that led to the deaths of hundreds of African Americans:

If we must die, let it not be like hogs
Hunted and penned in an inglorious spot,
While round us bark the mad and hungry dogs, . . .
Like men, we'll face the murderous, cowardly pack,
Pressed to the wall, dying, but fighting back!

Hard Times ▪ In the 1930s the economy of the United States nearly collapsed. The Great Depression caused people to lose their jobs, their homes, their savings, and perhaps worst of all, their hope.

The Depression was an absolute calamity for African Americans. Between 1929 and 1932, the income of black families in Harlem fell by almost half. In some sections nearly two thirds of the schoolchildren were undernourished. By the end of 1931, more than 40,000 Harlem blacks were out of work. The human suffering was immeasurable.

For West Indians, there was no longer much reason to come to the United States. Why put up with racism when there were no jobs to be had? Immigration came to a virtual halt. In fact, more people returned to the West Indies than sailed for America.

After World War II, with the return of prosperity, immigration from the West Indies picked up. But in 1952 the United States enacted a very restrictive immigration law. It permitted only eight hundred immigrants a year from the entire West Indies. Not until the 1960s would West Indians once more be free to immigrate to the United States in significant numbers.

From renaissance to poverty: This photo shows Harlem children waiting to receive milk during the Great Depression. West Indian immigration to the United States declined as a result of tough economic times.

HOME IN AMERICA | 6

Every Labor Day a huge celebration takes place in Brooklyn, New York. More than half a million people fill block after block of Eastern Parkway, a wide thoroughfare that is closed to regular traffic for the day. The rich aromas of barbecued meat, cod cakes, and curried goat fill the air. At about noon a long, winding parade begins. Flatbed trucks carrying steel bands and calypso groups start moving slowly down the boulevard. Other trucks haul huge loudspeakers playing recorded music. Elaborately costumed marchers and revelers follow each truck, dancing to the throbbing, buoyant music.

It is Carnival Day, the day to celebrate the culture and traditions of the West Indies. Amidst the throng are those who themselves or whose parents and grandparents emigrated from Jamaica and Trinidad, Nassau and St. Vincent, the Grenadines, Grenada, Antigua, the Virgin Islands, and a score of other places in the Caribbean.

A New Wave of Immigration ▪ Since 1900, more than one and a half million immigrants from the West Indies have come

A symbol of rising West Indian presence and pride in the United States: People celebrate Caribbean culture by wearing brightly colored costumes for a West Indian Day parade in Brooklyn, New York.

to the United States. By far the greatest number have settled in and around New York City. Today, entire sections of Brooklyn and Queens are occupied by West Indian Americans. But New York is far from being the only place with a large West Indian community. Sizable numbers reside in California, Michigan, Illinois, and Florida.

A large part of this West Indian community has arrived in the United States since the 1960s. In 1965, Congress approved the Hart-Cellar Immigration Reform Act, a measure that ended many of the old restrictions on immigration to the United States. Almost at once immigration from the West Indies accelerated dramatically, as it did from Central and South America, Asia, Africa, and the Middle East. In 1970 the number of immigrants from Jamaica was ten times what it had been in 1962. By the early 1980s about 50,000 legal immigrants from the West Indies were entering the country each year.

The new immigrants came from a West Indies that had undergone tremendous political changes. After years of agitation and negotiation, most of the Caribbean islands had become independent countries during the 1960s. Independence came peacefully; Great Britain voluntarily relinquished its empire. In August 1962, Jamaica marked its independence with two weeks of celebration and rejoicing. On November 30, 1966, Barbados became a sovereign, independent state. In the 1970s the Bahamas, Grenada, Dominica, St. Lucia, St. Vincent, Antigua, and the Central American nation of Belize won their independence. Some of these new nations did not wish to sever all their ties with Great Britain, and so they became members of the British Commonwealth of Nations, an organization of former colonies who accept the British monarch as their head of state.

Political independence was no answer to the perennial problems of poverty and unemployment, though. The West Indies stayed desperately poor. In the mid-1980s, the national income in Jamaica was about $1,500 a year per person; on other islands it was less than that.

Recent immigrants to the United States have come from all segments of West Indian society. The poor, of course, have compelling reasons for emigrating and continue to arrive in the greatest numbers. But professionals and trained workers have frequently found their ambitions thwarted in the Caribbean as well. For them, no less than for poor peasants, the United States has meant a land of opportunity.

Making It ▪ Starting with nothing, many West Indians took whatever work they could find in the United States. "Jamaicans will work in a house, even if it's menial, just to get money," explained one immigrant woman. Traditionally, they have refused public assistance. "Why you think I come here, for the weather?" said a recent immigrant. "If I wanted to sit around on welfare, I would have stayed home!"

Those from the West Indian middle class had a considerable advantage in securing work and have had a major impact on their communities. At one time in the early 1970s, more than half of all the black businesses in New York were owned by West Indians, and a high percentage of the city's black doctors, dentists, and lawyers were from the Caribbean.

With economic success, many left the old neighborhoods. "I still attend church on 119th Street in Harlem," explained an elderly Jamaican immigrant, "but now almost nobody lives in that area. Most are older folks, like me, who come in from Brooklyn. The few young folks are all from Queens or Westchester or Nassau. [Westchester and Nassau are suburban communities.] They never see Harlem except on Sunday. It's that way with a lot of churches, clubs and so forth."

The West Indian community has had its share of problems. In recent years, large cities have lost many high-paying factory jobs—jobs that were once the immigrant's ticket to the middle class—and have seen them replaced by lower-paying positions

A West Indian vendor on Fulton Street in Brooklyn, New York. After an easing of immigration restrictions in the 1960s, West Indians came to the United States in increasing numbers. They changed the neighborhoods where they lived and worked.

FULTON STREET

With so many West Indian Americans living in New York, some of the city's streets took on an entirely new and unique character. In the space of a few blocks on Fulton Street in the Bedford-Stuyvesant section of Brooklyn, a pedestrian could see and hear the sights and sounds of

with little future. And violent crime has become all too routine. In the 1980s the peace and quiet of many middle-class West Indian neighborhoods was shattered by the blazing gunfire of gangs fighting wars to control the sale of drugs. The gang members were frequently young West Indians.

dozens of Caribbean nations, from those of the Rastafarians, a religious group from Jamaica, to those of emigrants from the island of Haiti. In 1985 the writer Paule Marshall described the lively avenue:

Fulton Street is the aroma of our kitchen long ago when the bread was finally in the oven. And it's the sound of reggae and calypso and ska and the newest rage, soca, erupting from a hundred speakers outside the record stores. It's Rastas with their hennaed dreadlocks [long, braided hair worn by Rastafarians] and the impassioned political debates of the rum shops back home brought onto the street corners. It's Jamaican meat patties brought out and eaten on the run and fast food pulori, a Trinidadian East Indian pancake doused in pepper sauce that is guaranteed to clear your sinuses the moment that you bite into it. Fulton Street is Haitian Creole heard amid any number of highly inventive, musically accented versions of English. And its faces, an endless procession of faces that are black for the most part—for these are mother Africa's children—but with noticeable admixtures of India, Europe, and China, a reflection of the history of the region from which they have come. [5]

Single mothers fresh from the West Indies suffered hardships as well. Many were burdened with the responsibility of having to pay the room and board for all members of their household. Less than a third received any form of financial help, either privately or from the government. Many were

58

West Indians
have extended
their influence on
a national level
and beyond. Shirley
Chisholm, born in
Barbados, blazed
trails in American
politics. Jamaican
singer Bob Marley
brought Caribbean
culture to the
world through his
reggae music.

simply trapped. They could not get a job unless they had child care, but they could not afford child care unless they had a job.

Building Bridges ▪ The differences between West Indian Americans and African Americans have faded. The distinctions are still recognized but are no longer as evident. Marriages between West Indians and African Americans, for instance, have grown more and more common.

The unity of West Indian and American blacks was apparent during the social revolution of the 1960s. In his heroic and successful challenge to racial segregation in the American South, Martin Luther King, Jr., was assisted by Bayard Rustin, a brilliant organizer whose father was West Indian. In 1968 West Indian American Shirley Chisholm became the first black woman elected to the United States House of Representatives, where she quickly emerged as a fiery and eloquent opponent of discrimination.

During the 1960s, African Americans dissatisfied with both politics and King's principles of nonviolence and integration turned to the West Indian American Stokely Carmichael who promoted the concept of "black power." Malcolm X, the inspirational Black Muslim leader, also traced his heritage to the West Indies. His mother, born in Grenada, had immigrated to the United States about the time of World War I.

▪ ▪ ▪

So it is that on Carnival Day in Brooklyn, West Indian Americans have every cause to celebrate their past and present. The rhythms of reggae music reflect the spirit of the islands. The lyrics tell about the life of the people, through good times and bad. This mixture of medium and message expresses the West Indian Americans, a people whose presence has become its own reward.

NOTES

1. From "West Indians in the U.S.," *New York Magazine*, August 27, 1990.

2. From Ira Lunan Ferguson, *Fantastic Experiences of a Half-Blind* (San Francisco: Lunan-Ferguson Library, 1982), pp. 9–20.

3. From John C. Walter, *The Harlem Fox* (Albany, New York: State University of New York Press: 1989), p. 29.

4. From *Philosophy and Opinions of Marcus Garvey*, Amy Jacques Garvey, editor (New York: Reprints of Economic Classics, 1967), pp. 118-23.

5. From Paule Marshall, "The Rising Islanders of Bed-Stuy," *New York Times Magazine*, Part 2, "The Worlds of New York," April 28, 1985.

MORE ABOUT WEST INDIAN AMERICANS

Brothers, Don. *West Indies*. New York: Chelsea House Publishers, 1989.

Hicks, Nancy. *The Honorable Shirley Chisholm: Congresswoman from Brooklyn*. Scarsdale, N.Y.: Lion Books, 1993.

Lawler, Mary. *Marcus Garvey*. New York: Chelsea House Publishers, 1988.

Mason, Antony. *The Caribbean*. Englewood Cliffs, N.J.: Silver Burdett Press, 1989.

Ramdin, Ron. *West Indies*. Milwaukee, Wis.: Raintree Steck-Vaughn, 1991.

Springer, Eintou P. *The Caribbean*. Englewood Cliffs, N.J.: Silver Burdett Press, 1988.

INDEX

Page numbers in *italics* refer to illustrations.

DATE DUE			